AN ARK OF KOANS

[UOAP] THE UNIVERSITY OF ALBERTA PRESS

Illustrations by JACQUES BRAULT

AN ARK OF KOANS

E.D. BLODGETT

Published by
The University of Alberta Press
Ring House 2
Edmonton, Alberta T6G 2E1

Copyright © 2003 E.D. Blodgett
A volume in *(cuRRents)*, a Canadian literature
series. Jonathan Hart, series editor.

NATIONAL LIBRARY OF CANADA
CATALOGUING IN PUBLICATION DATA

Blodgett, E. D. (Edward Dickinson), 1935–
An ark of koans / E.D. Blodgett.

ISBN 0–88864–404–3

I. Title.
PS8553.L56A86 2003   C811'.6   C2003–910208–4
PR9199.3.B54A86 2003

All rights reserved.

No part of this publication may be produced,
stored in a retrieval system, or transmitted in any
forms or by any means, electronic, mechanical,
photocopying, recording, or otherwise, without the
prior written consent of the copyright owner or a
licence from The Canadian Copyright Licensing
Agency (Access Copyright). For an Access
Copyright license, visit www.accesscopyright.ca or
call toll free: 1–800–893–5777.

Printed and bound in Canada by Kromar Printing
Ltd., Winnipeg, Manitoba
∞ Printed on acid-free paper.

The University of Alberta Press acknowledges the
financial support of the Government of Canada
through the Book Publishing Industry Development
Program for its publishing activities. The Press also
gratefully acknowledges the support received for
its program from the Canada Council for the Arts.

 Canadä

for my children
and theirs

the Holy Trinity
Anglican Chancel Choir
(for the pencils, at least)

Timothy Findley
(for The Wars, *especially)*

à Jacques Brault
(qui a frayé le chemin)

and Irena (who fostered them)

CONTENTS

Elephants 2
Dogs 2
Firefly 3
Geese 4
Carp 5
Fox 5
Frogs 6
Sparrows 6
Coyotes 7
Sloth 8
Ants 9
Owls 9
Mice 10
Snail 10
Hummingbirds 11
Butterfly 12

Cranes 13
Dragons 13
Crows 14
Horses 14
Waxwings 15
Moles 16
Turtles 17
Wolves 17
Spiders 18
Bees 18
Herons 19
Trilobites 20
Cats 21
Nightingales 21
Whisky Jacks 22
Cows 22

Unicorns 23
Dolphins 24
Salamander 25
Swans 25
Minnows 26
Moths 26
Camels 27
Raven 28
Lambs 29
Phoenix 29
Prairie Dogs 30
Peacock 30
Penguins 31
Whippoorwill 32
Sheep 33
Robins 33
Bat 34

Bears 34
Dragonfly 35
Snake 36
Whales 37
Buffalo 37
Ducks 38
Vultures 38
Swallows 39
Mourning Dove 40
Rabbits 41
Eagles 41
Blackbirds 42
Locusts 42
Lions 43
Worms 44
Monkeys 45
Spruce Hens 45

Larks 46
Loons 46
Mockingbird 47
Dove 48
Voles 49
Terns 49
Donkeys 50
Falcons 50
Mayflies 51
Seals 52
Shells 53
Deer 53
Moose 54
Sea Gull 54
Pelicans 55
Birds 56
Bluebirds 57

Salmon 57
Faun 58
Osprey 58
Unicorn 59
Thrush 60
Roosters 61
Lynx 61
Polar Bears 62
Gazelles 62
Toads 63
Phoebe 64
Badgers 65
Cobras 65
Dinosaurs 66
Snails 66
Cuckoos 67
Envoi 68

AN ARK OF KOANS

No one can say goodbye
    to elephants, their heads
are yesterdays, the sky
    where they are in their beds.

Dogs come always out
    of nowhere, before you know
if they have come, a shout
    goes up and there they go.

A firefly is air
    alive with minor keys
of moons. Breathe with care—
    tides turn on your knees.

Goodbye. Goodbye. Goodbye.
  Geese turn their quills
against the mordant sky
  dancing with codicils.

Under the bridge a carp
    rippled the water: tears
of music from a harp,
    silence disappears.

The russet dancing of
    the fox swiftly turns
to flee from sight: above
    a leaf in silence burns.

The eyes of frogs are so
    steeped in peace that all
the saints must rise and flow
    from them without recall.

Even if they could,
    sparrows never depart—
their poignant feathers would
    impale the winter's heart.

Of coyotes all you see
 is what they let you think:
if you catch one, he
 will vanish in a wink.

The sloth is so slow
   that time seems to delay
before letting him go
   along his ageless way.

The intricate steps of ants
    mark fugues upon the ground:
no matter how light the dance
    earth you hear resound.

Owls are the shades of night
    floating into dark, and we
put on the moon, the light
    waning over the sea.

Mice departing leave
    nothing behind on the snow:
tracks of silence weave
    apart in tremolo.

Dreams of a snail go round
    the sun in spirals. It thinks
eternity its ground.
    It wakes: the cosmos shrinks.

Hummingbirds refrain
 from sleep: they leap into
the sky where they attain
 the stars to sip their brew.

The sleeping butterfly
 dreams of us it is said,
and when it does, the eye
 of God is our bed.

Cranes are flying against
     the moon: they seem to pause.
It is the world condensed
     to one, sudden cause.

Greater questions call
     for dragons as reply:
they are the sun, the fall
     of stars across the sky.

Crows in silhouette.
    Fragments of the night
put out the sun: we forget
    that they are birds in flight.

Horses came into sight
    arising from the deep:
far in the prairie night
    nostalgia makes them weep.

All the waxwings possess
    a mind to see the sun,
and seeing it seen say *yes*
    in muffled unison.

Moles in their helplessness
    work beneath the sod—:
impossible to guess
    they are the guides to God.

Turtles carry their home
    upon their backs. The there
of where they choose to roam
    is here inside the air.

No greater sadness tears
    apart the boreal air
than cries of wolves at their prayers,
    all grief laid bare.

The music of the spheres
    is heard by spiders: when
they weave webs, it appears
    in transmuted specimen.

Wisdom of the bees
    comes forth in Sanskrit—old
and deeper than the seas,
    only essence told.

Herons step with care
　　across the shore: they weave
into the sand their bare
　　calligraphy and leave.

The trilobites have left
    the absence that we sense
beside us, so bereft
    of other recompense.

Where is the soul to find
    its truest orient
if not within the mind
    of cats, when they consent?

When nightingales begin
    to sing, their song the stars
awakens with their din
    to call the other stars.

When whisky-jacks come down
    from trees, they make their nest
in souls, laughter the crown
    that they put on the blest.

Pacific seas that fall
    so gently on the shore
shine through the eyes of all
    the cows upon the moor.

When unicorns lie down
    to sleep, they seek a place
where girls spread out their gowns,
    and what lies down is grace.

Dolphins seem to raise
   aloft the waters of
the world: flesh is praise
   enough, its leaping love.

The salamander dreams
    of fire, heaven's light,
transmuted by the gleams
    of sunset, their delight.

Swans do not go to death
    in silence, they rejoice:
to sing with their last breath
    a god assumes their voice.

Sunlight on the lake
    dances in the shallows
lighting up the wake
    of silent, laughing minnows.

Sufis learned to dance
    by watching the moths turn
circles in a trance
    unafraid to burn.

All the mysteries
   of continents are placed
on camels: toward the seas
   they move without haste.

A raven stood alone
    against the farthest sky
and light upon him shone,
    but black: he made no cry.

The gambolling lambs leap
    so high into the air—:
they are joys that keep
    the world from despair.

Nothing more gnomic than
    the phoenix: it would mark
the cosmos with its span
    of life, its light and dark.

How graceful through the air
    are prairie dogs when they,
returning to their lair,
    pause suspended midway.

Who has not seen the eye
    of God who stares from where
the peacock lifting high
    his tail explodes the air?

Saints standing near
 the edges of the world,
their bearing as austere
 as penguins, wings unfurled.

One whippoorwill began
 to sing, the night fell
apart and stars ran
 down the sky pell-mell.

When everything seemed over,
    sheep were standing still,
heads at rest in clover
    as if it were God's will.

Spring is not the turn
    of suns in fresher skies
but robins who return
    to take us by surprise.

Through the summer night
    a bat casts music on
the world, taking flight
    upon its antiphon.

Winter enters bears
    slowly, and they assume
the sleep of earth, their lairs
    the spring in its womb.

Motionless above the stream
a burning dragonfly
had paused as if in dream
then melted in the sky.

The snake that lies in dust
    is silence to the eye:
in its parting, a gust
    of silence passes by.

The dreams the Vedas hold
    lie at rest within
the minds of whales untold
    where all the seas begin.

The great sun on the low
    and darkening hills comes down
upon the buffalo
    to rest in a small crown.

The last horizons are
    the flocks of ducks as all
vanish and from afar
    we hear the cosmos call.

Lords of the ruined skies,
    vultures brood in the trees,
waiting for the dead to rise
    and greet them on their knees.

If grace is infinite,
  swallows, then, before
God commanded light
  to be, were first to soar.

After the flood, the few
 who heard from down below
the mourning dove were too
 amazed to answer O.

Rabbits underneath
    the moon beatify
the air above the heath
    drawing nigh the sky.

Eagles sit enthroned
    upon the highest peaks
of stars, worlds disowned
    and bare beneath their beaks.

How can the innocence
    that blackbirds bring into
the world without pretence
    leave any residue?

Locusts came and went:
    if there are plains in hell,
the grasses there are bent
    and held beneath their spell.

Above savannahs the sun
dreams of majesty
where lions rise and run
in bright hyperbole.

For worms the earth poses
    no impediments:
their movement but discloses
    all its innocence.

When the clouds broke,
    monkeys came leaping down
from trees: in one stroke
    heaven tossed off its crown.

Spruce hens when they go
    become both leaf and light,
disappearing so
    into immortal flight.

How they rose in the skies,
    the little larks, and when
their song began, the eyes
    of heaven shone forth *amen*.

How could we forget
    the loons who touch the lakes
in spring and not regret
    their long, autumnal wakes?

The wanton mockingbird
    appeared to light upon
a hedge: heaven was heard
    in shining antiphon.

After the rain the world
 opened as a dove:
the music that unfurled
 we were not dreaming of.

Things that were too small
    to carry voles have swept
clean before them, all
    that was forgotten kept.

Leaving only for
    returning, terns are they
who round off, no more
    mere birds but fate at play.

Where donkeys walk along
 the margins of the sky
the air is fresh with song
 of saints before they die.

Falcons are possessed
 by silence: when they care
to fly, they take their rest
 upon it, emptying air.

How swift the mayflies come
    and go, no trace to find
on lakes, residuum
    of nothing left behind.

Seals take up their play
    between the elements,
dropping from the day
    their art of innocence.

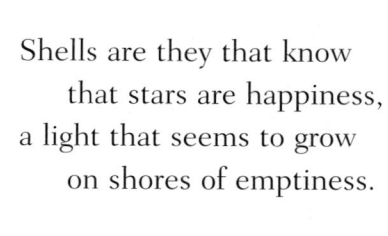

Shells are they that know
    that stars are happiness,
a light that seems to grow
    on shores of emptiness.

When deer descend to death
    the light of falling stars
goes out inside their breath,
    the air choked with scars.

Divinity is in
    the air where moose pass by,
each an origin
    of all that cannot die.

Only for a moment
    does the seagull's cry
break apart the silent
    grandeur of the sky.

Unbelievable
 the wakes of pelicans
on still waters recall
 the pomp of old pavans.

Epiphanies are so
 sudden the last cry
of parting birds echo
 before them as they fly.

They fall upon the air,
    the bluebirds from the south,
and take the shape of prayer
    inside an emptied mouth.

Dancing salmon split
    open the skin of streams:
ecstatic they submit
    to falls the cosmos dreams.

Thinking their dreams their own,
    every graceful faun
stands so alone
    beneath the first dawn.

All the beauties of
    the world lie below
the osprey hung above
    in slow intaglio.

Not once the unicorn
    can stand in any eye
that has not yet been born
    beneath a sacred sky.

A thrush was calling from
    the heart of spring: the trees
that heard were overcome
    with green mortalities.

Roosters on the shore
    of heaven waited for
the sun to come before
    they cried *excelsior*!

The eyes of lynx are all
    the stars that burn between
the trees invisible,
    as if they had not been.

Polar bears but seem
    to be the snow asleep
possessed by one dream
    that spring cannot keep.

No eternity
    is able to contain
gazelles in jubilee
    who dance above the plain.

The eyes of toads are great
   wells of sadness: where
do they gaze but into fate
   to see nothing there?

What does the little phoebe
	hope that she will find
crying *phoebe, phoebe,*
	always before, behind?

What is the kind of spell
    that badgers hide before
they don their masks? The smell
    of flowers, nothing more.

Like queens going away
    waving their last goodbyes
the stately cobras sway
    into receding skies.

Before the dinosaurs
    were gone, their angels must
have passed on through the doors
    of heaven into dust.

Snails go round inside
    a universe of their
making where they abide
    beneath the stars they bear.

Destiny is a ring
    of circles through the air
where all the cuckoos sing,
    scattering echoes there.

Invisible, they seem
    to sleep inside a stone
so silent only the dream
    they dream makes them known.

OTHER BOOKS OF POETRY
Published by the University of Alberta Press

Apostrophes II: through you I
E.D. Blodgett
0–88864–304–7
$14.95 paper

**Apostrophes IV:
speaking you is holiness**
E.D. Blodgett
0–88864–352–7
$16.95 paper

Bloody Jack
Dennis Cooley
0–88864–391–8
$19.95 paper

**Completed Field Notes:
The Long Poems of Robert Kroetsch**
Robert Kroetsch
0–88864–350–0
$19.95 paper

The Hornbooks of Rita K
Robert Kroetsch
0–88864–372–1
$16.95 paper

A Map of the Island
Nigel Darbasie
0–88864–371–3
$16.95 paper